The 10 Co

Coaching High ~~School Basketball~~

by Ken George

Dear Coach,

If you're like me, you can't stop thinking about basketball and coaching. You draw plays on napkins in restaurants. You pause NBA games after a good out of bounds play. You take a day off on the first day of the NCAA Tournament. If you're like me, your brain doesn't stop thinking about ways you can get more out of your team or more out of your assistant coaches. If you're like me, this game has brought you to tears more than once.

I was hired in 1994 to coach the Forest Hills Central boys basketball team. I first cried that day when I called my dad from the athletic director's office when it was official. Yes, the AD was right there watching. I cried when I called my girlfriend (now my wife of 23 years) from a pay phone a mile away from campus, and I cried when I walked in the door to my apartment in Albion where Meggan waited with a congratulatory cake.

I cried again 24 years later after my last game as head coach. Nobody but a few close friends and family knew I was done, but my son Jordan and I wept together in an empty gym about an hour after that district loss.

Now, the emotions connected to my coaching career make me want to tell stories. I teach English and journalism and have always been a writer. So, I've begun to write down my experiences as a coach so that I can share them with basketball junkies, coaches, and players.

The 24 years of coaching varsity basketball might be the most visible coaching I've done in my life, but I also coached youth baseball for about 10 consecutive years. For many of those seasons, I coached both sons who played on separate teams—this meant three to four practices and four to six games in the same week.

Beginning with tee ball and ending with the 8th grade all star teams (and throw a little travel ball stint in there), I'm guessing I coached 10-15 separate teams during this time period. Without a doubt, managing these teams taught me a lot about coaching, but mostly that many of the same methods I used to build a team with my varsity basketball program could be repeated with these groups and have a similar effect. The differences were many—younger players, shorter season, fewer practices, and a wider talent differential—but the strategies I borrowed from my varsity basketball program were similarly effective and rewarding for the kids and me. And, these methods led to success in terms of wins and losses but also in giving kids positive experiences.

I also coached AAU basketball for a couple years. Anyone familiar with AAU basketball knows the reputation is a free-wheeling, undisciplined game with players who are looking out mostly for themselves. For the years I coached AAU, I guarantee you that my teams did not fit the mold —sure we played fast and even frantically sometimes—but we were cohesive, emotional, and goal-oriented.

All of these coaching experiences have shown me that, in many regards, coaching is coaching. Regardless of the variables and obstacles, your goal is the same: **mold the group into a motivated, high-achieving, emotional, and cohesive team.**

My books will look at coaching from a basketball perspective, but regardless of the sport, I believe these 10 Coaching Commandments serve as the foundation for success. This book will focus on each commandment and give examples within each section. As you read, I invite you to use the self-assessment sections at the end of each chapter to evaluate your coaching philosophies. I believe that if you focus on utilizing these 10 tenets, your coaching (and the results) will be effective and enjoyable, and you will feel greater buy-in and commitment from whatever team you are coaching.

I hope you enjoy the book.

Coach George

COMMANDMENT #1: Identity

Have a consistent plan and sell that vision

In 2001, my 7th year as head coach at Forest Hills Central, I knew that I finally had a team that was talented enough to win a championship. We were young, but these players had come up through the system, and we had the pieces to compete with anyone on our schedule. Our first two games were against tough opponents, and we lost them both. Then, we outplayed a talented team for our first victory of the season. We were 1-2 and frustrated with our record when we headed to Hastings for a non-league game that we all knew we should win. Hastings was a smaller school than ours and was not a basketball powerhouse; they were known, however, for being a gritty and competitive team. Coach Don Schils always had his teams prepared. We were much more talented and should have won the game. But, from the very start, Hastings was more aggressive and desperate. They had one player—I still remember his name—who made shot after shot all night. In the end, we were beaten 83-57 by a team with far less talent. It was humiliating and an indication that change was needed.

I will never forget that bus ride home. I seriously considered quitting. I was doubting myself and my career choice. I had spent countless hours over the past seven years trying to build a championship culture, and my most talented team ever was 1-3 and on the brink of disaster. On top of that, I was exhausted. My personal life was busier than ever. I had two young children, a challenging teaching position, a wife who deserved more of my time, and a new house that we had just moved into. I thought maybe coaching wasn't for me.

Deep down, I knew the problem. We weren't different. We were just like every other high school basketball team—or any sports team—for that matter. I decided on that bus ride home that we needed to find a way to differentiate us and how we played from every other team on our schedule.

So, on that bus ride home, I made two decisions: first, we were going to focus on a pressure/denial defensive philosophy and second, we were going to call ourselves "Rangerball." The next day at practice, I gathered the team and explained that we needed to play our way. We needed to play "Ranger" ball. Then, to break the huddle, I said "Rangerball on three… one, two, three…" and the team repeated "Rangerball." On that day in the old gymnasium, a championship program was born. It was the day that changed the program forever. We went on to win several championships in the next 17 years and became known in West Michigan as one of the premier basketball programs.

Basketball is a pretty simple game when it gets down to it. You try to score while stopping your opponent from scoring. But, the intricacies of this process are multi-dimensional and innumerable. Deciding how your team is going to play and what your program is going to stand for is the first step in having a plan. To be effective, this plan cannot be confusing, haphazard, or inconsistent.

The first step is to simplify. Deciding what you want to focus on in your program or with your team is usually pretty simple. Look at what you notice about other teams and programs you see on television or live. Look inside your heart at what you think is most important in life and in basketball. Then, look at your situation and see if what you want to focus on makes sense. I imagine you probably already know what you want your program or team to stand for before you even read this sentence. Just make sure you simplify because your plan should lack ambiguity and be able to be stated in one sentence.

Here are a few examples:
- We are going to be fast, strong, and explosive and physically impose our will on our opponents.
- We are going to shoot a ton of threes.
- We are going to show class and humility in everything we do.
- We are going to out-prepare and out-execute everybody we play against.
- We are going to play multiple defenses to confuse our opponent.
- We are going to improve the skill set of every player in our program through workouts.

You can see that these plans are usually a combination of on-court and off-court qualities. By no means is your plan a catch-all for everything you'll do as a program. But, the overall plan should provide a hook or a big picture for everyone associated with your program to hold onto. You've probably heard of the "elevator pitch." Well, imagine yourself in an elevator with someone who asks you what your program or team stands for. You should be able to start with your one-sentence plan and then expand on it for no more than 20 seconds. When that person steps out of the elevator, he should know your plan. He might not believe in it and could have a totally opposing viewpoint on how things should be done, but he at least should understand clearly what your vision is for your team or program.

If your elevator pitch sounds like this, you have a problem:
"Well, we were 12-8 last year due to injuries so we had to play some zone, but I don't teach a lot of zone so we never got very good at it. I didn't think our JV guys were ready for the varsity style of play, so we played a lot of older kids who weren't that talented. We didn't have any good shooters this year, so we struggled to score unless we were pressing and getting layups. Next year, I think I'll be able to play 10 guys or so and be a faster team who plays more in-your-face man to man rather than pack line. We'll see. Every year is a different year."

This plan sounds like no plan at all. I understand that your talent level will change every year—you don't coach at Kentucky. So, it makes sense that you'll have to tweak your system and make adjustments all the time. But, if you don't stand for something and have a clear plan, I bet your elevator pitch sounds like the one above way too often.

After the disappointing loss to Hastings, I began to use the term Rangerball to describe our in-your-face defensive style and our offensive philosophy of playing as fast as we could and shooting a lot of threes. The style of play and this term—Rangerball—gave these guys something to work for and something to separate themselves from other teams. We had t-shirts made that said Rangerball, and I made sure to break every huddle and start every practice with this term.

Suddenly, the guys believed they were different. They believed they were part of a group that worked harder, prepared more specifically, and played more together. They went into every subsequent game that season

6

thinking we had won the game before it was played. We won seven in a row after that game and 16 of our last 17 games. We finished second in the league that year, but the foundation was built for a championship season the next year.

It is your job to build a brand with your team. Look at the most successful college teams over the past several years, and they all have something they are known for. Take this brief matching test to prove that this is true. Match the team on the left with the "identity" on the right.

1.	Michigan State	A. Talented freshmen
2.	Kentucky	B. High/low offense
3.	Syracuse	C. 2-3 matchup zone
4.	Virginia	D. Matchup zone, full court pressing
5.	Louisville	E. Packline defense, patient offense
6.	Kansas	F. High scoring transition offense
7.	North Carolina	G. Hard-nosed man to man defense

If you follow college basketball, this is not a difficult test. Is it any wonder that year after year these programs are at or near the top of their league standings and usually make deep runs in the NCAA tournament? Each of these teams and coaches stands for something. They have a way that they play that has become their brand. I believe the brand goes beyond just the style of play, too.

Part of MSU's brand is four-year players and the Izzone. Part of Duke's is Christian Laettner, Bobby Hurley, JJ Redick, and now Grayson Allen— players who were and are uniquely despised by fans and players from other schools. And part of Kentucky's brand was outlined in Calipari's book called "Players First." Come to Kentucky, and I'll let you showcase your talents for a year before you go to the NBA. As controversial as it may be, you can't argue with the success that program has had. It's their brand.

What's the lesson from this test? Well, if you're going to have a championship culture and build something that sustains itself over time, you need an identity.

Choosing how you're going to play

As high school coaches, we know that we don't get to choose our players. Some of you might disagree with this statement considering all the crazy school-jumping that has been happening lately.

But, generally speaking, high school coaches coach the players who grow up in their district. You can't recruit long, athletic players who would excel in a zone like Jim Boeheim does at Syracuse. You can't recruit big men who can shoot it like John Beilein has done to fit his offensive system at Michigan. Your players are your players because of where they live. So, can you play a certain system and then mold your players to fit the system? Or, do you need to change your style of play every year to fit the players on your team that year?

The answer lies somewhere in the middle. You can certainly build a program that relies on full-court pressure and teach your players to outwork your opponents. But, if you have a slow-footed, unaware player who happens to be the best shooter to ever come through your school, you had better find a way to fit him into your system. Adjusting to fit your personnel is absolutely necessary, but without a doubt, you can define a way that you're going to play and use your best players within that system.

Once the plan is established in your mind, it is time to communicate that plan to your team and those close to the team like your assistants, managers, and athletic director. This isn't done through email or with a handout. Your plan is communicated through the consistent, repetitive, and pointed actions you begin to take. Having a plan for your team is similar in a lot of ways to having a plan for your own children. You can tell your kids that the plan is you can't use your phone after 10 p.m., you need to be at family meals, and you have to read 30 minutes a day. That's a great plan. But, telling them that and actually matching your actions to that plan are very different. Until your actions match this plan, your son or daughter will be sitting in his or her bedroom late at night on Snapchat after missing the family dinner without any idea what a book even looks like.

Your actions will depend totally on your plan. Let's take the first example from before:

"We are going to be fast, strong, and explosive and physically impose our will on our opponents."

This plan could be the entire basis for a successful varsity basketball program for 20+ years. The defensive and offensive systems the team uses might vary slightly from year to year depending on personnel, but the plan from the head coach is that this program will focus on being "fast, strong, and explosive." From day one—and then consistently for as long as you run the program—you need to stick to this plan with your actions (and words) to make it the basis for everything else you do.

So, step one would be to set up a weightlifting and agility program yourself or through your school's strength coach. Step two would be to focus part of every off-season workout on strength, speed, and agility. Even ten minutes out of an hour workout is enough to communicate that your plan is intact, important, and invariable. Step three would be to make sure that all of your players understand that an empty spot in their schedule during the school year should be filled with a weightlifting class if your school offers one. Lastly, you would need to ensure that part of every in-season practice focuses on improving your players' bodies. This would be true for every level within your program: freshman, junior varsity and varsity.

My program's plan could be summarized in this sentence: "We are going to shoot a ton of threes, deny every pass, and out-prepare our opponents." Of course, this plan didn't come to light until about halfway through that bus ride in year seven. Up to that point, the program was somewhat successful, gaining momentum, and providing some exciting basketball for the community. We were winning more than the program did the few years before, the guys were committed and together, and the coaching staff and players were working very hard. But the results were still inconsistent overall—a direct result, I believe, of an inconsistent plan.

That day in 2001, I decided on a plan, named it "Rangerball," and began to sell that plan to everyone involved. That changed everything.

The second part of the first commandment is "sell the vision." Having a plan in place is one thing, but convincing others that it's the right plan might take some work. Sometimes, wins and championships can do that for you, but before those happen on a consistent basis, you have to essentially become a door-to-door salesman with your players and the people connected to your program.

Start with the first group that has to buy into your plan: the players. Consistently communicate your plan to them. Sometimes come right out and say it; other times, communicate it subtly and stealthily. Your players will sense your excitement and belief in the plan based on your words and actions. Mention examples to them of other players, teams, and programs who have had success with a similar vision. Praise players who put in the work necessary to support your plan.

For instance, with our plan of shooting a lot of threes, we always had groups who would get together and spend hours on the shooting machine in the gym. When players put in extra time shooting, I made sure to mention it publicly when all the players were together. Even a subtle mention of a player putting in extra time shooting often led to other players asking for more gym time. Over the past 15 years, my players put in more time shooting on that machine (we have gone through a few of them) than you could imagine.

Our plan was based on shooting threes and a pressure defensive system. My belief was that anyone could play in the defensive system with the right coaching and a high level of effort. So, while many of my players lifted weights as part of a class or for other sports, until the last two years of my coaching career, we didn't do as much in the weight room or with agility or explosiveness. We spent our extra time shooting. In the last two years, however, our school implemented a required team lifting/agility program so my teams worked with our strength coach quite often.

The focus for me, however, continued to be shooting, shooting, shooting. I'm sure other coaches in the area would say that their number one concern before playing us was defending the three point shot.

The next group to sell the plan to is the parents and community. This process should happen naturally as your plan takes shape. The parents will see what your focus area is because their son or daughter will be involved in the extra shooting, lifting, etc. Once your team hits the court and demonstrates your plan, the community can start to buy into the system and see that you have a vision for the program. Winning isn't a necessity early on, but playing with emotion and energy and a system is. Too often,

I've watched an entire basketball game and still had no idea what one team's plan was—almost invariably, that team lost.

Have a plan that you believe in. Take steps to initiate that plan and make it known. Then, sell that plan to everyone associated with the program. Even in a losing season due to a lack of talent, injuries or a tough schedule, if you have a plan and sell it, your program will still move forward and take steps towards winning championships.

Things to consider:
1. **If you asked five of your players to write down the top three things your program stands for, would they repeat most of the same principles?**
2. **Can you explain the basics of your plan in 30 seconds or less?**
3. **Do you do the extra things to give your plan the basis for success?**
4. **If someone watched one full practice and one full game, would your plan be clearly evident?**

COMMANDMENT #2: Delegate

Give up power to your assistants and leaders

Over the past 24 years, I've had a variety of situations in terms of assistant coaches. For the first ten years or so, I coached alone at the varsity level. I don't exactly remember why I never hired an assistant in those early years, but my control issues and budget constraints were probably the main reasons. After those ten years, my typical coaching situation became one full-time assistant along with a part-time younger assistant coach who was usually a former player. In my final season, I was blessed with three assistant coaches. One thing was constant, though: my assistant coaches were given power and responsibility.

I will be the first to admit that I have control issues in my classroom and as a head coach. I like things a certain way and tend to do whatever necessary to ensure they happen as such. As I became a more confident and veteran coach, I realized that controlling every single situation was not only overbearing, but it was unnecessary. So I began to look at ways to delegate power to my assistants, captains, and the team as a whole. As soon as this became a more regular occurrence in the program, I noticed a more intense and committed buy-in from everyone involved. Now it was *their* program, too.

My practices always started with a team huddle at half court. I was rarely the main speaker in the huddle. In fact, most often, I never went into the huddle at all, and the first time I would officially address the team each day was after about thirty minutes of actual practice time. The pre-practice huddle was reserved for the captains and occasionally an assistant coach. I figured the players get enough of my voice during practice, so if I could limit the talking before we got going, they might be more receptive to my coaching later. I always took into account that these kids had just spent the last eight hours sitting in desks mostly listening to teachers talking.

Giving your captains or leaders opportunities to be in charge isn't as hard as it seems. My captains and leaders were in charge of the pre-practice huddles, pre-game captains' meetings (these took place at halftime of the preceding game), and pregame fire up huddle (when we went back into the locker room in the middle of warm ups). They also played key roles in our team meetings when we did book club and handed out reward stickers.

I will explain more about the book club and reward stickers in a future book. Sometimes, depending on how your captains are chosen, one of your team leaders won't have the captain title. In this instance, you need to find opportunities for him or her to be in a position of leadership.

In my last season of coaching, the final fire-up talk in the locker room was given every game by a senior non-captain. He was the voice of our team in a lot of ways—my two captains were outstanding leaders and two of my best players and captains ever—but this other player had a way of firing guys up. So, when we went back into the locker room with ten minutes remaining in warmups, he circled up the team and gave a brief motivational talk before our final huddle. Often, I didn't even go into the locker room for this. It was their time to be a team and to see that I wasn't the one pushing them to be excited to play. They were excited for and with each other.

I see four key advantages to delegating power.

1. Assistant coaches feel more important and committed
One day after I resigned after twenty-four years as head coach, I began my career as a varsity baseball assistant coach. Immediately, the head coach gave me input into how practice would run and even put me in charge of the post-practice conditioning and cool down. Even though it was his first year as head coach, he clearly understood the importance of making your assistants feel valued. From day one, I was committed to him and his program because he showed the trust in me to take over part of practice.

A valued and committed assistant coach is a better assistant coach. My assistants helped with scouting and game planning and were certainly an important part of every practice. What was the result? They were more engaged overall and more likely to make constructive comments and adjustments that helped the team succeed. If your assistant coaches spend most of practice just watching and making a comment here and there, I urge you to rethink how you're utilizing them.

2. Players motivate each other
I often asked my teams what would happen if I was absent from practice for the first thirty minutes or so. Would practice start at the correct time? Would our typical pre-practice and early practice routines be followed? Would the effort and focus levels be the same as if I were there? When

you think about it, your presence as the head coach should have little to do with the approach from your players. If the only reason they are working hard is because you are there and watching, then you have larger issues than what offense and defense you're working on.

As you give your players more ownership, you'll see that players hold each other accountable and begin to motivate each other to give their best effort, be on time, and stay focused. This is when you really start to build a championship culture. So, giving your players these opportunities will lead to a more easily motivated and more focused team.

3. Coaches and players become a united front
When assistants are given key roles in practice, the continuity within the coaching staff is enhanced. This continuity is important to getting the most out of your team. Every few years before an important game, I talked with my assistants and my team about one of the biggest advantages we had going into that game: continuity. I'm sure you've seen teams who are not only playing against their opponents, but they are also essentially competing with their head coach and assistants at the same time. It's a lot to ask of a group of guys to rally around each other and not only beat the other team, but to do it while lacking trust and belief in their own coach.

In these situations, when it comes down to a big play or the last few minutes, it always seems like the team who is more trusting and together wins. Giving your assistants and players opportunities to lead brings everyone together as a trusted and trusting unit.

4. Gives you a chance to step back
Being the head coach is hard work. If you're reading this book, you probably already know that. It's physically challenging and mentally exhausting to be in charge of everything at every moment. In my last several years of coaching, it was enlightening and refreshing for me to step back and give up some of the control. When my players started running the pre-practice huddle, I was able to meet with my assistants about my goals for that day. When my assistants were running breakdown drills in practice, I was able to take a step back and watch through the lens of an outsider who could evaluate all aspects of that practice at that point.

I don't remember ever missing a practice in all my years as head coach. I'm pretty sure I left 10-15 minutes early a couple times—once for a doctor's appointment for my wife when she was pregnant with my second son and once or twice to get to a middle school game that one of my sons was playing in. Other than those rare instances, I was there and involved. Stepping back and allowing others to take the lead sometimes gave me a chance to take a deep breath while still being present and involved.

Things to consider:
1. How often do you allow your assistant(s) to be in charge of a meeting, drill, etc.?
2. Would your players consider you, your assistants, and them a united front?
3. Are your players motivated by each other?
4. Do your assistants feel like a vital part of any success you and your team have?

COMMANDMENT #3: Brevity

Say less, but say it more often

We've all been guilty of it at some point. We huddle the team up and begin to go over just a couple key things. Then, the one-minute talk turns into three minutes. Then—yep, you guessed it—three becomes five becomes ten. Anyone who has attended after-school staff meetings knows that any speech that lasts more than five to seven minutes is listened to about as intently as the story that is told for the tenth time by that weird uncle at your family get-togethers. It's over. Nobody is listening.

Coaches are teachers even if that's not their day job. Coaching is teaching. And, teachers love to hear themselves talk. So, as coaches, we have to understand and be empathetic of our athletes' situation. They are at practice to be active and engaged and physical. Sitting in desks all day is tough on a teenager; sports practice is their chance to get moving and active. Long, drawn out, repetitive talking from a coach usually does nothing to motivate, energize, or inspire your players to compete at their best level.

Planning an effective practice and even pre-game routine is an art. There are ebbs and flows in any day, meeting, practice, and game. Long talks (anything over two minutes) rarely improve the flow and intensity of the practice. I would guess that many high school basketball practices start with the players huddled around the head coach for a five to ten minute talk about the previous game, the upcoming game, or even the plan for the day's practice. Why? The contents of this talk should be split up into several short bursts of information or intensity or inspiration rather than doled out in a lengthy sermon before the kids are loose or mentally and physically engaged in practice. I would argue that the same words said at the start of practice would have much more impact spread throughout practice at opportune and appropriate times.

The "say less" rule should be followed in just about all situations. Of course, there are a few times each season that a longer talk may be necessary, but I would hope that even a 20-minute team meeting to air out some issues wouldn't be 20 straight minutes of the head coach talking. Saying things briefly and succinctly will lead to a more receptive audience every single time. If you stick with this commandment, the next time you ask for their attention and begin to expound on how terrible they are at transition defense, your players will be much more likely to listen closely because they know the speech will be meaningful, targeted, and most importantly, short.

Once you start to make the change to say less, make sure you remember the second part of the rule: *say it more often.* Interrupting the flow of practice with coaching is a necessary but dangerous proposition. I was always most concerned with intensity and energy in practice—it's impossible to work on execution and schemes if your players are not intense and energetic. Rarely did we do one drill for more than five minutes, and rarely did I stop practice and talk for more than two or three minutes at a time.

But, any of my former players and assistant coaches would tell you that I didn't allow a lack of effort, intensity, or execution to go uncoached. Likewise, tremendous or inspirational effort, intensity, or execution was often singled out and praised. So, I stopped practice (or spoke through the transitions between drills) regularly, but tried to make sure that I never heard my own voice for more than a couple minutes and even asked my assistant coaches to time me to make sure most of my comments and teaching points were communicated in thirty seconds or fewer.

We all know that saying something doesn't mean it's going to be heard and listened to. It's a two-way street. So, as coaches, we need to do everything possible to make sure our audience is receptive. Talking more often, but in shorter bursts, is a great first step.

Things to consider:
1. **Do you start or end practices with a talk longer than five minutes?**
2. **Do you notice your players' attention (eye contact, body language, etc.) fading during your instruction?**

COMMANDMENT #4: Outwork

Do extra and then talk about it

Joey Saladino, now a police officer in Grand Rapids, is one of my all-time favorite Rangerball players. He is most famous for one thing in our program: morning shooting.

Joey has an award named after him that is given out at every banquet because I have never seen a player put in more time working on his craft. Joey was a shooter. More specifically, Joey *made* himself a shooter. And, along the way, he made me teach with bags under my eyes. The first text would come at about 9 p.m.

"Hey coach. Can you rebound for me tomorrow morning?"

I had such a love/hate relationship with these texts.

My head said, *"No, Joey, I will not get up at 5:15 tomorrow to rebound for you because I am exhausted from coaching, teaching, parenting, watching tape, grading, etc."*

My heart (and my texted reply) said, *"See you at 6"* every time.

Until last year, Joey held the school record for most threes in a game with nine and still holds other three-point shooting records. He did extra. And, I talked about it all the time. I am convinced he made so many shots for two reasons: first, he made himself a great shooter, and second, he actually believed that he *deserved* to make every shot because of all the extra time he put in.

His morning shooting was the impetus for me to make a point to do extra whenever possible and then to talk about it later. These things gave us an edge. They gave us a reason that we should win. They gave us belief.

As a program, we did a lot of things that could be considered *extra*:
- Team book club every preseason, during which we read chapters, took quizzes, and discussed as a team
- Two-day, off-campus team retreat in the preseason immediately after team selections

- Team notebooks were used every day with scouting, plays, motivational notes, etc.
- I wrote every player a personal note before every game with three individual goals
- Large sticker boards with each player's picture on it; stickers were awarded the day after games for goals reached, wins, diving on the floor, etc.
- Thursday night team meals at my house
- Rangerball gear purchased by parents and given out at a special team-only event at the retreat
- Quizzes over game tape
- Morning shooting. Evening shooting. Weekend shooting.

This is not everything, but the list gives you an idea of some of the traditions within our program. I'm sure all coaches are doing more than is required, and this list isn't meant to show that I worked harder or longer than any other coach. I'm sure I didn't. But, I made a point to have the guys do many things together that were outside of just coming to practice for a couple of hours every day and then playing on Tuesday and Friday nights.

My pre-game talks were usually pretty brief—more on this in Commandment # 9—but many of them contained the same message: "We have done more, prepared more, and worked harder than our opponent. We have earned the right to win this game. Now let's go do it." I was able to convey this message only because of the extra time our players, coaches, wives, and parents committed to the program.

Sun Tzu said in his work *The Art of War* that "Every battle is won or lost before it is ever fought." Similarly, most athletic contests are over before they begin either because one team is just too talented to be beaten by a much lesser opponent or because when two similar opponents come up against each other, one of them has done extra and prepared more to win.

I tried to make sure that we were always that team.

Things to consider:

1. Are you doing enough "extra" that you can talk about it with your team?
2. Do you feel you go into many games as the more prepared team?
3. What is one little extra thing you could do this season that might give your team a better chance to win one game?

COMMANDMENT #5: Consistency

Control and minimize slippage

Slippage is easily defined by looking at a familiar situation we have all been a part of: the first day of school. On the very first day, everyone walks in on time. Everyone sits quietly (and awkwardly) while the teacher mispronounces nearly everybody's name. Then, students listen intently while the teacher talks for quite a while about class rules, expectations, etc. Nobody asks to go to the bathroom for the entire hour. At the end of class, everyone waits for the bell and exits in a neat and orderly fashion.

Now picture the fifth day. Or, the fifteenth day. Or, the fiftieth day. Or, if you really want to analyze slippage over time, look at the last day of school.

As time passes, slippage starts to occur in the classroom if the teacher allows it. Some students periodically start showing up late, they ask to go to the bathroom during class, they lose focus during lectures, and they start to head to the door five minutes before the bell is due to ring. All of this slippage is the result of one thing: the teacher allowing it little by little.

As a coach, you must fight against slippage *every single day*. If your team does some sort of pre-practice stretching, this is the first place you'll probably notice slippage. We got away from stationary stretching later in my career, but if your team sits in a circle around a captain to start your practices or workouts, you need to control and manage this situation to minimize slippage.

On the first day, everyone is counting together, doing the same stretch at the same time, and clapping in unison after every stretch. As days go by, the circle gets sloppy, the counting quieter, and the clapping grows less enthusiastic.

This is slippage — and slippage in your pre-practice stretching sends this very clear message to the players: slippage is acceptable. If slippage is fine in your pre-practice routine, then how can you expect your players to execute their plays correctly or appropriately handle defending a ball screen?

Slippage is natural in all aspects of life for most of us, so fighting it with your team is going to take focus, energy, and commitment. Your players will naturally tend toward slippage because that is what they are used to in their classes, with their families, and with every other sports team they have played on. This makes slippage even more difficult to fight and means it is critical that you fight it every day.

Here are some of the key places slippage happens:

1. **Team notebooks:** On the first day, everyone has it with them, and it is organized and neat. By the second week, someone forgets it. By the third week, some of the notebooks start to look beaten up and disorganized. I constantly fought slippage in this area during my career. We ran for missing notebooks, and I made a point to use them nearly every single day of the season so the expectations were clear. We sometimes had binder organization days to refile all the scouting, game report cards, etc. into their appropriate locations.

2. **Gear:** We required every player to wear his team-issued practice jersey every day. But, one player was bound to forget his during the second or third week of the season. When this happened, the entire team ran. Every season, some players wanted to warm up without their practice jersey on. They would try to have it sitting on the side to put on when our pre-practice routines were over. Our coaches didn't allow this. Everyone wore their practice jersey from the start to the end of practice. No exceptions.

3. **Time:** Ask any of my former players about me and being on time, and you'll get two reactions: first, an eye roll, and then, a mention of "Rangerball Time."

    Slippage in punctuality is a team-killer because it's usually your best player(s) or your oldest players who start to push the boundaries on this. As soon as your best or oldest players are allowed to be late, you've lost credibility with your team. "Rangerball Time" is a term that my players started attaching to my obsession with being early. Open gyms scheduled for 7 p.m. started at or before 7 p.m. The first game was usually underway by 6:50. If players wanted to have a chance to be in the first game, they arrived by 6:30. Practice always started with group stretching five minutes before the published time. A 7 p.m. practice meant a 6:55 stretch as a group. Getting there at 6:30 was the norm. You cannot allow slippage in being on time.

4. **Execution of the little things:** As the season wears on, players (and often coaches) start to take short cuts on executing the little things. A focus area early in the year—let's say the intricacies of "jamming the ball screen"—gets less attention later in the season because of the focus on scouting reports and other critical areas. If you allow slippage in how the ball screen is jammed in practice, then there is no way you can expect correct execution in the game. There is always a natural drop off from practices to games in doing the little things correctly. So, slippage on a screen angle, ball screen defense, or play memorization late in the season in practice will undoubtedly lead to a mistake in the games. Your job is to stay consistent in your expectations from the first day until you are knocked out of the state tournament (or win it). This focus on the little things will trickle down to your players and execution will stay as sharp as possible.

Things to consider:
1. **Are you allowing slippage in pre-practice routines?**
2. **Are you allowing slippage in some other area—attire, time, etc.?**
3. **Are your older and better players showing slippage in the little things?**

COMMANDMENT #6: Inclusion

Coach everybody

The title of this section seems obvious, but over the years of watching coaches and teams of all sports and levels, I have seen this commandment neglected more than any. When I say "coach everybody," I'm specifically addressing two different situations:

1. In-game or in-practice coaching of a specific skill or situation
2. Season-long coaching of every single player on your roster

Here is an example to explain the first situation: it's the middle of practice, and the team is competing in controlled up-and-down scrimmaging that requires the defense to get two "stops" before they can play offense. In this drill, a player does a poor job of setting his man up before using a flare screen that is part of a play set. So, the coach blows the whistle and approaches the player to explain his error.

Situations like this one present themselves over and over in every practice, and coaches can react in a variety of ways. If you really want your player to correct his error and not repeat it for the remainder of the season and his career, you need to do some direct teaching here. How you do the direct teaching is vital to your team's success later.

In situations similar to this one, I've seen coaches blow the whistle, approach the offending player, and take some time to privately explain and demonstrate the correction to that player while the 10-14 other players stand idly losing focus, staring blankly ahead, or even beginning to take a couple shots and pass the ball around. This coach is making an already difficult task (coaching) more frustrating.

His goal is clear, and the fact that he's willing to stop practice to quickly and directly correct the player is admirable. But, his approach is setting himself up for many frustrating coaching moments later that season.

Later in the season, a different player makes the same error in a game, and the coach turns to his bench and angrily yells, "I went over that in practice! Why can't we set our man up for that flare screen?" Yes, the coach did go over it in practice, but he only taught it to one player.

It is crucial that coaches engage every player when they are specifically addressing a key point in practice. It could be defending a ball screen, running transition, fronting the post, or boxing out on a free throw. Each of these situations, and the other 10,000 situations that we attempt to cover in practices, is experienced by all players. Therefore, if you want execution to be handled a certain way, everyone needs to be listening during the instruction.

Use the volume of your voice, your body language and posture, and an insistence that all eyes are on you when you teach. And, of course, follow Commandment #3: say less. Many times in practices, I began my teaching in a situation like this by loudly emphasizing "All eyes on me!" Then, instruction of the execution would be brief and direct.

On most teams, in any 5-on-5 situation you use in practice, a few players will be sitting out because most teams will have 12-15 players. These players not directly involved in the on-court playing should be walking with the play (moving up and down the sideline as the play goes from end to end) and listening intently when teaching occurs.

Too often, I have seen coaches teaching the ten involved in the play while the three players sitting out are getting a drink or even just taking shots on a side hoop.

How can a coach expect all of his or her players to execute something that has been emphasized only to a select few? This makes no sense. If all players don't hear the instruction, then the coach will absolutely end up repeating himself later.

The second part of this commandment focuses on your role as a coach for all of the players on your roster.

Rosters include all types of players: those who play most of the game, quiet players, role players, leaders, captains, "cool" kids, friends, beginners, etc. For a varsity team, you can add the variables of younger kids pulled up, seniors who don't play much, three-sport athletes, and players who rarely see any game action at all.

Each of these players needs to be coached. I do not believe that you can or should coach any two players the same way. The old adage *treat all players equally* is a falsehood. Sure, you need to hold all players accountable to the same standards, but how you get there with each player depends on variables only you as the coach can see. Any good teacher knows how to get the most out of each of his students. Coaching is the same. Some players need to be verbally pushed to excel. Others need you to praise and then correct. Still others have personal situations that require you to take a different approach. But, the fact remains that every single player needs you to be his coach.

It takes a purposeful and planned approach to coach role players or players who rarely play. In the first 10-15 years or so of my coaching career, it was easy to find players who were excited to just be a part of the team with no concern for the number one issue with parents: playing time. I still had many of these types of players in my last ten years of coaching, but they were a little bit rarer than earlier in my career.

One of my greatest (and most humorous) memories of coaching is when I decided to keep a minimally talented player who would be a perfect complement to the rest of the team in so many ways. He would be the 15th player on a highly-talented 15-man team. I was returning all five starters from a 19-3 team, and we were expected to have a championship season (we ended up going 22-1 and losing in the quarterfinals to Saginaw High School with Lamar Woodley from the Pittsburgh Steelers and Anthony Roberson from the NY Knicks). When tryouts concluded, I began my one-on-one meetings with each player in my office to either keep or cut and to briefly explain why. Matt walked in apparently expecting to be cut because when I told him I'd like to keep him as a 15th man who would rarely if ever see game time, he literally fell to the floor in disbelief and relief.

He was lying on his back saying "Thank you, thank you, thank you" on the ground in my office in front of my assistant coach and me. It's a story I told often to my teams as an example of commitment to the team and selflessness. Coaching Matt—and the 75 or so other players during my career who rarely saw game time—required me to have empathy for their situation.

Let me start this explanation by making sure you don't think I was "soft" with these players or demanded anything less from them than my top players each season. What it took to be a Rangerballer didn't change if you were an all-state player or the last guy on the bench. Expectations were expectations and everyone was held accountable. But each player was not coached the same way. As this section of the book emphasizes, however, players who rarely saw game time received just as much attention (good or bad) as the top players. Coaches cannot allow anyone on the team to feel less valued.

How to do this really depends on your program and your personality. I used a variety of methods to let these bench players know that they were important to the success of the team as our all-league players.

1. **Personal notes**: As mentioned previously in this book, I wrote a brief personal note to every player before every game and handed it to him when we gathered to watch the JV game or have our captains' meeting. The notes were only a few sentences and always ended with their three personal goals for that game. In these notes, I reminded the role players of their importance to this team. Most of the time, their individual goals for games were not about their own play in that game. For instance, they would look something like this: *1. Tyler* (one of our starters) *makes two three point shots 2. Team is ahead after first quarter 3. Official has to warn our bench to sit down - bench warning for too much energy.* These notes and goals gave me an opportunity to show these players that I thought about them and saw their role as critical in the big picture.

2. **Pre-game bench huddle**: Just as the starters huddled briefly on the court after starting lineups were introduced, my substitutes also huddled prior to the tip. In the first couple of games, my assistant coach or I would start the huddle and talk briefly. After a few games, the players huddled without us and got fired up for the start of the game.

3. **Private comments**: I made sure to talk to every one of my players privately once a week all season. Even if this was a one-minute talk prior to stretching at the start of practice, that was enough to keep our relationship close and let them know that they were on my mind. I did this with all fifteen players every season. I'm sure I missed a player or a week here and there, but I consciously worked hard to have these very brief conversations all season with every

player. For the bench players, this one-minute explanation of what I've noticed from them in practice or meetings let them know that I was indeed watching them and thinking about them just as much as the star players.

4. **"White Squad" meetings**: Each year, the players who were not in the top six or seven became known as the "White Squad" because they wore the white side of our reversible practice jerseys in practice. In some of the seasons where we had many close games in a row, a few players on the "White Squad" could go two or three weeks consecutively without getting in a game. When this happened, I made sure to spend a couple minutes after one of our full-team meetings to meet with the White Squad as a group. In this brief meeting, I would thank them for their commitment, let them know that I knew it was difficult to not play in games, and remind them of the commitment they made to the team when I decided to keep them on the team after tryouts despite the chance of a limited role in terms of game time.

With some concerted effort on your part, all 12-15 players on your team will be motivated to fully commit themselves to your plan. Coaching everybody is a crucial piece of this effort.

Things to consider:
1. **Do *all* of your players hear *all* of your explanations in practice *all* of the time?**
2. **Are you doing things to keep your bench players involved and valued?**
3. **Do you take a couple minutes at least every other week to have an individual talk with every player?**

COMMANDMENT #7: Timing

Pick your spots

If you've ever been in a committed relationship with a significant other, then you are already familiar with this commandment in that setting. Over my 23 years of marriage to the love of my life, I've learned to pick my spots when Meg and I have a different point of view on an issue. Sometimes, after careful consideration, I just move on and leave this decision alone. Other times, I try to discuss the decision further and work to convince her that we may want to pursue a decision that is slightly different than her specific plan.

As a coach, picking your spots is difficult, but I would argue that coaches who don't follow this principle end up talking (or yelling) at their players more and being heard less.

Coaches make decisions about picking their spots constantly, but in this section, I want to focus on a few specific situations:
1. Pre-game motivational speeches
2. In-practice yelling/challenging/motivating
3. In-game yelling/challenging/motivating

Pre-game motivational speeches
As mentioned earlier, my pre-game talks were very brief and usually focused on the few things that we had pinpointed as keys to winning during the days leading up to the contest. It was an opportunity to reemphasize what we talked about and worked on in practices and meetings prior to game night. The actual "fire up" portion of the pre-game was left to the seniors, captains, and leaders.

Each season, however, I ended up giving three to five emotionally charged speeches before certain games. I have to confess to any former players reading this book that while many of the speeches may have seemed spontaneous, there was usually a plan (usually days ahead of time) for me to get emotional and fiery.

That's not to say that any of it was fake. I think my former players would describe me as an emotional coach. So though I knew ahead of time what my focus was going to be in these pre-game speeches, the emotions that came out during the speech were very real.

Choosing the games to give these emotionally-charged talks usually took place before the season and took several factors into account. First off, I rarely used a motivational speech before a game that I knew my team would already be on a high for like crosstown rivalry games, tournament championships, district or regional games, or games against highly-ranked opponents. The players didn't need me on these days to get the juices flowing. These games were some of my favorite to prepare for because I knew that I could focus on the Xs and Os of winning the game without having to worry about my team's energy and emotional investment.

Most often, I used these motivational talks before Tuesday night league road games when we were the favored team or non-conference games that would impact the momentum and mindset of our team and season. This is when our fan base would be a bit smaller, the bus ride would be a little longer, and our opponent would be looking to seize the opportunity for an upset. These are the games that win conference championships. I believe that many coaches make the mistake of focusing on (and building up the emotion for) the games that are already highly important to the players. On these nights, the players, parents, and fans don't need the help.

Although you should expect great effort and focus for every game your team plays, you know that you cannot have your players at their highest emotional level for every game. So, pick your spots for your pre-game motivational talks.

In-practice yelling/challenging/motivating
Your players hear your voice a lot. When you include open gyms, lifting sessions, conditioning, meetings, and practices, your voice is more prevalent in their lives than any other voice, including their parents. This is dangerous because your voice can become mundane and lose its impact. Your players can begin to *hear* your voice but not actually *listen* to it.

Hearing is the physical ability for players to sense the noises your voice makes. You want your players actually *listening* to your voice with their heads and hearts. Therefore, you need to pick your spots during practice. Instead of looking for more opportunities to talk to my teams, I looked for ways to avoid using my voice while still getting information across. This is the main reason for the pre-practice captain or assistant coach meeting. Often, I spoke ahead of time with my captains or assistants about something I wanted them to focus on in that meeting. It's why I always worked to say less but say it more often. It's why I wrote a pre-game note to every player instead of meeting with them. I did everything I could to make sure my voice didn't become white noise to my players.

This requires some conscious work on your part during practice. You need to think of ways you can chunk information into one brief talk or what can be saved for later. You need to think of what results are most important to you and focus on those before you give lengthy speeches on unnecessary topics. You need to be empathetic to your players who have been hearing your voice since the first day.

Again, I want to stop here and emphasize that this does not mean you need to be "soft" in your approach and let things slide. That's not what I'm saying. The point is that you need to understand that your main goal is for your players to hear your voice, listen to what you said, and then utilize that information to improve their play. This cannot happen if your voice is as constant in their ears as the Snapchat notifications on their phones. The impact of your words and ideas will be lost if you don't pick your spots in practice.

In-game yelling/challenging/motivating
Now that I have resigned as head coach, I have picked up officiating as a way to stay involved in the game and give back to the basketball community. In the summer, I officiated more than 100 games in team camps, AAU tournaments, and scrimmages. Being on the "other side" has been eye opening in many respects, but one behavior by coaches has stuck out to me more than any other. I am shocked by the number of coaches who essentially "announce" the entire game for their players.

Many possessions sound like this example that starts with an opponent's free throw attempt and ends with giving up an open three-point shot in transition:

"Box out!"
"Good rebound."
"Look up."
"Don't dribble! Find a guard."

"Push it."

"Don't force it!"

"Set it up!"

"Get to your spots."

"Run it!"

"Stop standing!"

"Cut! Move!"

"Take him to the hoop!"

"That's a bad shot!"

"Get back!"

"Who's got #12!"

"Stop the ball!"

"Where's our help?"

"Close out!"

"Time out!"

If you read this to yourself just now and thought for a moment that it sounds a bit too familiar, then this section of Commandment #7 is for you. Announcing the game to and for your players is the best way to make sure that your voice ends up as white noise. If your goal is to be background noise and for your players to play scared and timid, this strategy is perfect for that outcome.

Announcing the game does nothing to empower your players to play with flow and confidence. Can you imagine someone doing this to you while you tried to accomplish a somewhat difficult task?

As I write this, I'm trying to picture someone standing behind me saying "Good sentence! Now add another example. No! A different one. You need a comma there—why did you use an em dash?" Ridiculous, right?

Well, this behavior by coaches in some of the games I officiated over the past couple months is equally ludicrous. Coaches need to pick their spots to use their voices during games. All of the information contained in the quotes above needs to be taught and emphasized in practice so you do not have to tell your players to react accordingly during games.

Two specific situations from the last couple of months stick out to me as examples. First, I officiated one game where the coach yelled, "Close out! Choppy feet!" on *every single close out* for an entire game. I could not believe it. I'm sure he said it close to 250 times during that one-hour summer scrimmage. You could tell he was a very good coach because of how his players competed, and they definitely closed out well. But there is no need for him to yell "Close out! Choppy feet!" every time one of his players comes from help or rotates to guard someone. I'm sure his players do not even hear it any more. He certainly could be using his time and voice differently.

The other situation is a team that did three things extremely well without any prodding or reminding from the coach who sat quietly on the bench the entire game. This is a veteran coach who runs a specific system and has won many championships at this small school. After just a couple minutes into the game, it was obvious what he focused on in practice. First, on every single defensive transition, all five of his players pointed to a man and verbally announced whom they were covering. The consistency of this never wavered. It happened on every single possession for the entire game including any time the other team substituted. Immediately, all five players would point and talk about their matchups. He never yelled "Match up!" once during the game.

Secondly, his players turned and found someone to box out on every shot by their opponent. The coach never yelled "Box out!" during the game, yet his players boxed out on every possession.

He obviously had coached this, emphasized this, and practiced this prior to this game. I imagine many of these players had been doing this in his youth camps for several years.

Thirdly, when he needed his team to foul to stop the clock so he could put in another group of five players, he didn't stand up and yell "Foul!" or "Get him!" All he did was say a code word in a normal tone of voice, and one of his players would instantly foul (they were also obviously taught to go for the ball), allowing him to substitute. I am sure this situation played out exactly the same way late in games during their season when they needed to foul. It was practiced, planned, and focused on. He didn't need to overuse his voice to get this result.

Coaches need to pick their spots in games to give their players instructions. Announcing the game leads to confusion, a lack of flow, and athletes playing while looking over their shoulder or waiting for the next instruction. Rarely does this lead to successful play.

Things to consider:
1. Do you notice yourself "announcing" the game?
2. Are you trying to give a "Fire Up" speech before every game?
3. Do you sense too often that players are hearing your voice but not really listening to it?
4. Is there more you can do in preparation for games so that you can use your voice when necessary rather than constantly?

COMMANDMENT #8: Communicate

Communicate openly, honestly, and often

Over the past few months, I've run into a number of people who have congratulated me on my 24 years of coaching and asked why I resigned. Most of these conversations start with a suggestion from them that I left because I was tired of dealing with parents. Nearly everyone thinks I resigned because of parental involvement. This might be because some coaches complain frequently about parents and how they are over-involved in their kids' lives. Or, it might be because Twitter and Facebook are always active with stories of parents who write or say ridiculous things to coaches, or maybe even because of stories of athletic directors who let coaches go because a group of parents is rallying against them.

Dealing with parents had nothing to do with my resignation. I just wanted to try some new things in my life now that I'm 50 and both of my sons are in college. I definitely had some parent issues during my 24 years of coaching, but I also believe many potential issues were avoided because of open communication.

First off, we have to understand that no parent will ever be able to understand fully the situation we are in as coaches. They cannot look at the team and season without bias because they have a son or daughter involved. The only people involved in the program who can look at the team without any preconceived notions or biases are the coaches (unless their child is on the team).

Knowing up front that your parents will have bias means that you can take one of two stances: communicate openly and often with an understanding of this bias, or avoid communication with parents. I highly recommend Option #1 even though it will be uncomfortable and awkward at times. And, of course, it requires boundaries.

If you have children you have coached or who have played in any competitive athletic endeavor (even at a very young age), you know that you watch games differently when your child is involved. If you don't have children, I'm sure you can understand this angle from when you competed as a younger athlete and your family watched you play. It is important to understand this bias and then to openly communicate with parents through organized and controlled avenues.

About 15 years ago, I instituted one of the most important changes into my basketball program. I began to hold "player/parent/coach" meetings after every season before spring open gyms began. These meetings became the building blocks of a culture built on honest, open, and appropriate communication between the head coach and the parents. At the banquet, my players and their parent(s) signed up for 15-minute meetings that took place after school in my classroom in the couple of weeks between the banquet and Spring Break.

The meetings were for varsity basketball candidates, and I emphasized the importance of having the player and parent(s) in attendance. The meetings were one vehicle to open up communication between the parents/players and me, but they were controlled in terms of time and location. I had handouts ready for everyone, outlining what I saw that year, what the player needed to improve upon, and the summer camp/open gym/workout schedule.

The most important outcome of these meetings was that parents were thankful for the honest and open communication. The news they received certainly wasn't always what they wanted to hear, but at least they were informed and aware of where their son stood. For the players, it was an opportunity for them to hear what they needed to improve upon for the next season. Some of the meetings were pretty difficult, but I still believe the parents usually walked out of the room thankful for the upfront and honest communication.

This was just one example that kept the lines of communication open with parents. I also spent considerable time at the first parent meeting of the season talking with the parent group and with individuals about the upcoming year.

It was at this meeting that I let parents know that I would love to talk with them during the season—at appropriate times and in appropriate settings—about their son's situation on the team. I made it clear that texts, emails and phone calls were not to be sent or made within 24 hours of any game. And, I also made it clear that any concerns their sons had should be taken up with me first by the player. Then, if the parent also wanted to talk, I was open to that. Letting the parents know that it wasn't me against them made most seasons pass without any serious parent problems.

I also held an open practice early in most seasons; the parents sat in chairs along the sideline and watched the entire practice. I handed out practice plans to the parents with descriptions of each drill and spent time talking with the group during the practice about what drill we were doing at the time and the purpose of that drill. It was only two hours out of an entire season of practices, and the benefits made it well worth it.

In my last season, I invited all parents into the locker room for a game late in the season to hear my pre-game talk and watch us do our "Starting Lineup" tradition. This was just another way to let them know that I valued their place in the program and wanted to give them and their sons the best experience possible.

Open communication with players is equally important. As mentioned earlier, spending time in one-on-one conversation with each of your players at least once a week will let them know that you have their best interests at heart. That doesn't mean they will play more or that you will be any easier on them in practice. It just means that you are a coach who cares for his players beyond the basic coach/player level.

Players may not agree with what you have to say or your decisions about playing time, etc., but communicating often and openly with them will lead to more buy-in to your plan and goals.

Everything we do as coaches is for the betterment of the young people we work with. We are using basketball as a tool to teach them about life. For most of our players, basketball is something they do for fun and to be a part of a team.

Openly discussing their performance and their place on the team models important traits including honesty, compassion, and empathy. Teaching and modeling these traits in the highly competitive and emotional world of athletics is immeasurably important to the character building of the young people you work with.

Things to consider:

1. Do you have any organized or planned methods of communicating with parents?
2. Do your players really know where they stand and what they need to work on?
3. Do you make major changes in playing time, starting lineup, etc. without any real communication with the players involved?

COMMANDMENT #9: Reliability

Do not allow excuses or poor body language

We had some behaviors that were non-negotiables in Rangerball.
- *No profanity.*
- *No excuses.*
- *No negative body language.*

Everyone has his pet peeves. As a parent, it bothered me when my sons didn't hang up their towels in their bathroom after showers. As a teacher, I struggle with students who walk in right as the bell rings and want to get ready to leave a few minutes early. Coaches are the worst when it comes to pet peeves. I have too many to list here, but the ninth commandment of this book covers two of them: excuses and negative body language.

Making excuses is a learned behavior. In some families, children learn from their parents early on that nothing is their own fault. Rather, it is the teacher's, friend's, or coach's fault when things don't work out as planned. In other families, parents teach kids to take responsibility for their actions and to be accountable for the results. If you are allowing players to make excuses—or if you yourself are making excuses for your team—you are probably not on the path to a championship.

Basketball is a game of mistakes, and excuses are often quick to follow. Make a point early on in your season or in your building of a program that excuses will not be tolerated. My assistants and I fought the excuse culture pretty hard at the start of each season. The varsity players realized quickly that making excuses would lead to a stoppage of practice and a very brief running session. Here are a few examples of the types of excuses we typically encountered early in a season:

- "I got picked." - after giving up an open shot
- "It slipped." - after badly missing a shot
- "_____ wasn't where he was supposed to be." - after messing up execution of a play
- "Where was my help?" - after getting beaten off the dribble
- "Nobody is moving." - after over-dribbling or turning the ball over

Unless you are a first-time coach, you've heard these excuses and many more. It is important that excuses such as these are not tolerated from the beginning. If your players have a habit of making excuses, it's a pretty easy habit to break. Just don't allow it. When you hear one in practice, simply stop practice, acknowledge the excuse, emphasize briefly that excuses lead to a losing culture, do a brief down-and-back run, and move on. It won't take long for your players to understand that errors they make need to be owned. The words they say after mistakes will be "That's my fault" instead of "I got picked." I'm not a big fan of "My bad" because it can be said flippantly and maybe even sarcastically. But, it's better than blaming mistakes on other players, the rim, the scheme, or some other outside force that has nothing to do with what happened.

The second team-killer is negative body language. It seems like this was rarely talked about when I played in the 1980s in high school and college. But, with everything being recorded now, the importance of eliminating negative body language has moved to the forefront. We have all seen the pictures and videos of a player on the end of the bench leaning back with his jersey untucked and a look of disinterest on his face, and we are faced with an NBA right now that allows complaining after every call. A couple years ago, I thought the NBA cracked down on player reactions to calls, but the complaining is worse than ever. It is hard for me to watch. Unfortunately, our players watch, and the greatest players in the world are setting a pretty poor example.

Negative body language needs to be eliminated in the following instances:
1. When subbed for
2. On the bench
3. During timeouts
4. In response to coaching
5. After calls during games

If you allow slippage in negative body language, it will multiply very quickly and become common on your team and in your program. Much like eliminating excuses, teaching about body language should be purposeful and consistent early in each season.

For whatever reason, the best players are usually the worst with body language; that is a somewhat broad generalization but one that might ring true with you when you think about teams you have coached. If this is the case, address it seriously and immediately. Your best and oldest players need to be the models for the younger people on your team and in your program.

For the past several years, my assistants and I taught and practiced how to react in each of the above situations so that the players understood our expectations.

1. **When subbed for**: players run of the floor, slap five with the coach, get a drink, and come back to the seat *directly next to the coach*. They do not sit at the far end of the bench.
2. **On the bench**: players stand when a player comes off the floor and always sit leaning forward engaged in the game.
3. **During timeouts**: the players in the game sit, and the players not in the game go behind the bench and lean in closely facing the coach. I made this change to our timeout arrangement because the players behind me in a typical timeout setup cannot hear what I am saying, and I cannot see their eyes or gauge their engagement in the message. That's a problem because some of them will be in the game very soon.
4. **Response to coaching:** players look the coach squarely in the eyes and respond with a nod or a verbal agreement such as "Ok, coach" or "Yes, coach." Players know this expectation includes practices and games.
5. **After calls during games**: players hand the ball to the officials and do not make gestures of any kind with their hands and arms.

These are not the most natural reactions to the situations listed above, so some teaching is required. Once the players know your expectations, they quickly master the skills and respond appropriately. When slippage begins in these areas, a quick correctional run will reiterate to everyone that you are serious about your commitment to doing things the right way.

In the short term, excuses and negative body language can alienate certain players and some fans. In the long run, it leads to a losing culture. If your best players are looking to play in college, then positive body language is absolutely necessary. Many college coaches have told me that this is the first thing they look for when recruiting a player at a high school game or an AAU tournament. Teams who make excuses and have poor body language may win some games, but when things get tough and they face adversity, their lack of control will lead to losses and embarrassment. Therefore, it is our job as coaches to stop these behaviors before they become habits.

Things to consider:
1. Do your players know what you expect in terms of body language?
2. Do you practice and explain positive body language?
3. Are you making excuses for your players such as "We have a lot of injuries" or "Playing back to back games is tough?"
4. Can you do more to eliminate excuses?

COMMANDMENT #10: Balance

Balance the negatives with positives

Somewhere along the way, many coaches have learned that coaching should be an "angry" activity. I would argue that watching college basketball coaches may be at the root of this problem because if you haven't noticed, about half of the time while you watch a college basketball game, the camera is focused on the coach. College coaches have become very much the focal point of television broadcasts. Basketball games are stopped often for violations, fouls, timeouts, etc. Some of these breaks last five seconds while some last a couple minutes. One constant during these breaks is that the viewer gets a close look at the highly-paid head coach's reactions at that time.

Most often, the coach is unhappy or even angry. I know these coaches are not angry all the time in practice and meetings and other basketball events. I'm sure these coaches smile, laugh, high five, and hug their players when off camera. But, during these important televised games, how often do you see the head coach smiling, laughing, congratulating, and enjoying the interaction with his players and the officials? Rarely.

For the most part, we only see these coaches in game situations and rarely after a good play by their teams. Instead, the cameras focus on these coaches only when they are complaining, chastising, screaming, and imploring players and officials. I believe this has led to many high school coaches coaching angrily. Some coaches yell after turnovers, missed box outs, bad shots, and execution errors. On the good plays, they stand or sit quietly because that play went how it was supposed to go. That is what was supposed to happen, so a reaction isn't necessary. It seems like the opposite should be true more often.

Coaching angrily leads to very little satisfaction for anyone: the players, the coaches, the officials, and even the fans. Coaching angrily leads to players looking over their shoulders instead of playing with confidence. Coaching angrily leads to players leaving the sport or losing their desire and love of the game. Quite simply, coaching angrily is wrong.
I want to emphasize again that balancing positive and negative feedback does not make you a soft coach. I'm not saying that you need to over-compliment or lower your expectations for your players. I'm just

suggesting that if you spend more than 50% of your time complaining, questioning, or chastising your players, then you should make a change. Most of the people reading this book were basketball players at one time. Many of you probably played for multiple coaches beginning with your youth basketball experiences all the way to your high school or college playing days.

Do you remember why you starting playing the game in the first place? Probably because it was fun. You enjoyed playing the game.

Do you remember a season or game (or a coach) that made you lose the enjoyment of the game?

I'm sure some of you are picturing your high school coach. He or she yelled constantly. Every turnover led to an explanation of what you should have done (like you tried to turn it over). Every mistake was amplified because not only did you just make a bad play, but you also had to hear about it all over again from your coach. This coach might have even told you at some point to "Stop shooting!" or "Never dribble!" I am urging you right now to not be that coach.

During my officiating experience over the past couple months, I would estimate that about a third of the coaches in the games I worked coached "angrily."

I often felt bad for the players on the court who were playing scared, playing not to mess up, and playing without any enjoyment at all. I sadly watched some of these players lose their love of the game right before my eyes.

Playing for an angry coach does not improve performance. It might improve effort or intensity in the short term (out of fear), but it does not lead to better passing, shooting, or ball handling. These activities require skill and practice and confidence. Being constantly yelled at actually makes executing these fine motor skills more difficult.

The power of praise is well documented in books and journals. You have probably worked for or around someone who is an expert at using praise to motivate. It is proven that workers or players who are praised for outstanding effort or execution or performance want to duplicate that situation again.

Most likely, you have felt this in your playing career. You dove on the floor for a loose ball. Your coach praised you for the effort. What happened the next time a loose ball came your way? You dove again, of course.

As the head coach and main influence on your players, you should infuse praise into your coaching and resist the urge to coach angrily. This is not to say that you can't "pick your spots" and go off on your team. We have all done it, and it is appropriate and necessary at times.

As mentioned earlier, I was an assistant for our varsity baseball team this season. With a few weeks remaining in the season, the team was struggling a little with excuses and focus. I asked the head coach if I could "go off" on the guys before a Saturday tournament as a way of getting them to refocus and toughen up for the adversity we would face in the tail end of our season.

With his blessing, before our morning game one Saturday, I took the team behind the outfield wall and sat them down.

For about 10 minutes, I coached angrily. Rarely did I publicly call out individual players in my coaching career, but I did it here.

Then, I challenged all of them to toughen up, quit making excuses, come together, and rise up as a group to make a run at a state championship. There was no praise—it was all yelling and all angry for a solid ten minutes or so. After the first of our two games that day, two players came up to me and said the same thing: "Thanks, we needed that."

I use this example to make sure that you understand that the positivity required to build a culture of success, buy in, and togetherness does not come at the expense of challenging your team when it is needed. You can coach more positively and still have a tough team and be a tough coach. If you believe that you are more than 50% negative as a coach in practice, meetings, and games, then I challenge you to adjust the ratio. Work towards a 50/50 split in your coaching and avoid "coaching angrily." Here are some tips to get you started.

1. Avoid knee-jerk negative reactions to turnovers and bad plays
Y at a player immediately after a physical error does nothing to prohibit that player from making the same mistake again or a different mistake soon afterward.

2. Smile and laugh in practice
It is absolutely appropriate to smile while coaching. If coaches pick the right spot that doesn't ruin the intensity or flow of practice, a good laugh does everybody some good.

3. Publicly praise extraordinary effort
This is the best opportunity for praising something that will influence future behavior by your team. Praising a made jump shot does not help future jump shots go in, but praising incredible effort leads to more incredible effort.

4. End practice early at least once a season for great effort and play
Players will be shocked. Happy. Excited. Maybe even confused. They will come back the next day ready to be back in the gym and wondering what other surprises you have waiting for them.

5. Avoid yelling at your bench players for plays on the court
This makes no sense. A player on the court takes a bad shot and some coaches turn to the players on the bench and yell, "We are always taking bad shots. Move the ball and make sure we get a good shot!" Players on the bench resent coaches for this behavior.

6. Avoid yelling general negative statements like "Why don't we ever box out?"
This also makes no sense and does not lead to any change in behavior. A team will not box out more if the coach screams loudly to nobody in particular after a missed box out.

7. In most cases, include positive and negative feedback to players
I'm not saying that coaches have to use the "sandwich" method every time they want to get on a player for something. But, adding in some positives when correcting a negative habit can only help motivate the player.

Things to consider:

1. Ask one of your assistants for an honest answer about your negative to positive ratio.
2. Do you yell at players after turnovers or bad shots?
3. Do your players usually play with a love for the game?
4. After watching you coach one game and one practice, would an outside observer say you love your job?

Dear Coach,

I hope this guide to ten keys to coaching has fired you up as you head into your next season of coaching basketball or any other sport. Your style and goals might not match mine, but I do believe that using these ten keys will help you have a more enjoyable and successful season.

Please look for my other books coming out in the future:
- *"The Championship Difference: 10 little things to get your team over the hump"*
- *"Coaching your own son or daughter"*
- *"Case studies: Specific games and what they taught me"*
- *"20 motivational ideas for your program"*
- *"Winning the special teams battle in basketball"*
- *"Practice planning, organization and drill ideas"*
- *"Dealing with parents"*

Visit kengeorgebasketball.com for more information or email Coach George at coachkengeorge@gmail.com

Special Thanks and Dedication

Special thanks to my wife, Meggan, for her motivation and energy as I tried to put my thoughts on paper and for all the behind-the-scenes work to make this book a reality. You amaze me in so many ways.

This book is dedicated to Jordan and Tyler George. When I began my career as a head coach, I had a dream to someday have a son and coach him. Well, I lived that dream twice and could not be more proud of your accomplishments as players. More importantly, I am honored to be the father of two humble, kind, talented, and trustworthy young men. You make me proud every single day.

- Head boys basketball coach Forest Hills Central HS (1994-2017)
- More than 350 career wins
- 9 league, 4 district, and 3 regional championships
- Past president of Basketball Coaches Association of Michigan
- WMOA Coach of the Year
- MLive Grand Rapids Coach of the Year
- Camp director:
    - West Michigan Guard Academy
    - HoopSmart Basketball Camp
    - West Michigan College Basketball Academy
    - West Michigan HoopSmart Coaching Academy

90667881R00029

Made in the USA
San Bernardino, CA
12 October 2018